YES LORD

I WILL FOLLOW YOU

PRAYERS / PRAISES / CRIES OF THE HEART

YES LORD

I WILL FOLLOW YOU

His Victory Publishing
Roseville, CA

Chris J. Fenner

HVP

His Victory Publishing, Roseville, CA
Yes Lord, I Will Follow You
Paperback 1st edition, August 2019
Updated, December 2021

Copyright © Chris J. Fenner, 2017

All Scripture quotations, unless otherwise indicated, are taken from the Holy Bible, New International Version®, NIV®. Copyright ©1973, 1978, 1984, 2011 by Biblica, Inc.™ Used by permission of Zondervan. All rights reserved worldwide. www.zondervan.com.
The "NIV" and "New International Version" are trademarks registered in the United States Patent and Trademark Office by Biblica, Inc.™

Cover photograph by Shutterstock
http://www.shutterstock.com/

All rights reserved
HIS VICTORY PUBLISHING
Roseville, CA
http://www.chrisjfenner.com/

International Standard Book Number
ISBN 978-0-9815419-6-9

Dedicated

to

Conrad & Katie

APPRECIATIONS

To my wife, Diana, who has faithfully journeyed with me in following Jesus, I quote the words of Proverbs 31: 29-30:
> "Many women do noble things,
> but you surpass them all.
> Charm is deceptive, and beauty is fleeting;
> but a woman who fears the Lord is to be praised."

To my good friend, Don Bleyl, for designing the illustrations at the start of each chapter, I say, "Thank you."

ENDORSEMENT

YES LORD I WILL FOLLOW YOU is a practical prayer guide for you to walk with our Lord. Chris Fenner allows us to learn from his walk with Jesus as he chronicles prayers and practical lessons spanning over 30 years of his life. This resource will greatly encourage your soul at times when you may not be able to find your own words.

DAVID KUBAL
President/CEO
Intercessors for America

CONTENTS

PREFACE	3
OUR GOD	
Who Is Our God?	8
Life Is As Simple As This	9
Great Is the Lord!	10
God's Power In Us	11
What Joy!	12
One Truth?	13
Entering In!	14
His Word	15
Your Word	16
WAITING & LISTENING	
Be Still	18
Crossing the Desert	19
My Complaint to God	20
Listen to the Lord	21
Wait for the Lord	22
Your Voice	23
My Will – His Will	26
WALKING WITH JESUS	
The First Easter	28
Abide in Him	29
His Peace	30
Our Choosing	31
Lead Me On	32
Jesus Is My Friend	33
Follow Me	34
Come Up Higher	36
You Are Too Wonderful	37

Jesus A to Z	38
Today's Reminders	42

OUR SIN & REBELLION

That I May Love You More	44
Cleanse Me	45
He Is Faithful	46
Turning Aside	47

FAITH & LOVE

Not Because I Am Able	50
Jesus Is Lord!	51
A Life of Faith and Love	52
Love Is...	53
The Wind of the Spirit	54
The Purpose of Life	55

PRAYER

Rejoice!	58
The Beautiful Gift of Prayer	59
My Prayer for You	62
A Prayer of Affliction	63
Prayer for Those Seeking the Truth	64
May I This Day...	65
Why We Do Not Hear from God	66
The Many Parts of Prayer	68
In Sickness & In Health	69

OUR NATION

A Plea for God's Mercy	72
O Lord, Heal Our Land	73
A Cry for Our Nation	74

WORK

My Workplace Prayer	76

The Blessings of Work	77
Alive With Christ at Work	78
The Joy of Business Travel	79
I Rejoice	80
His Presence	81

HIS CREATION

The Lord of All Creation	84
A Reason to Hope	85
The Bay	86
The Mountain Lake	87
The Birds of the Air	88
Come and See!	89
Majesty!	90
Not By Chance	91
Flowers of the Field	92
Two Truths	93

HIS VICTORY

His Victory	96
The Lord's Warriors	97
The Battle	98
Increase My Faith	99
Why So Fearful?	100
The Gift of Time	101
Gloom to Glory	102

PRAISE

Lord Most High	104
Rejoice, Rejoice, Rejoice!	105
Praise Him!	106
In This I Can Rejoice	109
I Sing to You, Lord!	110
What a Pilgrimage!	111

"Come, follow me," Jesus said, "and I will make you fishers of men" (Matthew 4:19).

YES LORD, I WILL FOLLOW YOU

PREFACE
How "Yes Lord, I Will Follow You" came to be.

I was brought up in a loving Christian family in Gloucester, England, and attended church twice each Sunday until the age of fourteen when my parents told me I could decide for myself whether to go to church or not. I immediately decided against church, as I found that it did not relate to real life. And when I went to college in London I became an atheist and joined the Humanist society.

I held this secular worldview until I was 39 years old as I pursued success in the world and climbed the management ladder in the oil industry. A reorganization of the company where I worked left me sidelined from the main business activity, however, and this precipitated the start of a midlife crisis. Shortly thereafter, the training manager at the company asked me to give a series of classes on the topic of motivation to other managers. These classes were very successful which prompted me to start writing a book on motivation.

I sent a book proposal to over seventy publishers and literary agents and received the same number of rejection letters. I felt it was important to write this book, however, and so I decided with my wife to leave the company where I was working and move to Santa Barbara, California to devote myself to writing and speaking on the topic of motivation.

After two months I realized that I had nothing worthwhile to write. Also, having cut my ties to the oil industry during a time of a severe downturn, there was no option of going back.

By this time the Lord had started to break down my wall of atheism through: the faithful prayers of my mother for 25 years, the wonderful example of Christian life by a manager who worked for me, and the powerful witness of the gospel message by a teenage missionary.

Then on the afternoon of August 27th, 1985 I took a walk along the Arroyo Burro beach at Santa Barbara, and, in desperation over the impasse I was in, I knelt down on the sand and prayed, "God, if You are there, please give me a sign!" I remember thinking how stupid such a prayer was, but when I opened my eyes, two sea lions lifted their heads out of the water—no more than twenty yards from where I was kneeling—and made eye contact with me. To me it was a really big sign!

My activities immediately changed from writing about motivation to seeking to understand Christianity, and I read avidly on the topic. Then in February of the following year I became ill with a severe respiratory infection and was in bed for a number of days. On the afternoon of February 13th I heard a voice that was clearly directed to me saying, "Chris, will you follow Me?" I discounted the voice as the effects of the fever, and thought nothing more about it until the following afternoon when I heard the same voice saying, "Chris, will you follow Me? I need to know."

Although I did not understand the full meaning of this "calling" I responded. "Yes, Lord, I will follow You."

This was the start of an incredible journey of following Jesus. We remained in Santa Barbara for

PREFACE

another eighteen months after which the Lord directed me back to the oil industry: restarting work in the industry exactly two years to the day from the appearance of the sea lions!

Why had the Lord made Himself known to me in such a powerful way through the vision on the beach and His audible voice? I pondered this question many times, and came to realize the Lord wanted me to have an intimate walk with Him in order to be an example to others that He is still the all-powerful, living God: the true God who is involved in every part of our lives—just as in the Old Testament stories and the New Testament gospel messages.

This book records prayers, praises and cries of the heart that have come to me over more than thirty years of following Jesus. They capture the peaks and valleys, the joys and anguish of what it means to follow Jesus in the glorious fulfillment of the purposes He has created us for. I hope the content encourages you to seek and find your own glorious journey with Him.

Chris J. Fenner
August, 2019

YES LORD, I WILL FOLLOW YOU

WHO IS OUR GOD?

Our God is an awesome God:
who reigns in heaven and earth; a God who created all the stars in the universe, a God who created the finest petal on an azalea in springtime.

Our God is a pure and holy God:
so pure and holy that our impurity, our sinfulness, is laid bare before Him; so pure and holy that we must have an intermediary—a redeemer, Jesus Christ, His Son—in order to come before Him.

Our God is a powerful God:
so powerful that there is nothing we can do for Him, and nothing He wants us to do for Him except turn our hearts wholeheartedly to Him, so that He may direct His power into the world through us.

Our God is a living God:
concerned about us and watching over us each moment of the day, so that at work, at home and in all our other activities we can know His will and His way.

Our God is a God of love:
so loving that He sent His son to earth to be killed by man yet to overcome death to act as a shepherd for us in heaven; so loving that, however far we stray and however long we are away, He is ready in an instant to welcome us back into His fold.

> For the LORD your God is God of gods and Lord of lords, the great God, mighty and awesome (Deuteronomy 10:17).

LIFE IS AS SIMPLE AS THIS

Look to Jesus.
"Here I am! I stand at the door and knock. If anyone hears my voice and opens the door, I will come in and eat with him, and he with me" (Revelation 3:20).

Turn to Jesus.
"Repent, for the kingdom of heaven is near" (Matthew 4:17).

Surrender to Jesus.
"For God so loved the world that he gave his one and only Son, that whoever believes in him shall not perish but have eternal life" (John 3:16).

Hope in Jesus.
In his great mercy he has given us new birth into a living hope through the resurrection of Jesus Christ from the dead (1 Peter 1:3).

Trust in Jesus.
"I am the vine; you are the branches. If a man remains in me and I in him, he will bear much fruit; apart from me you can do nothing" (John 15:5).

Rest in Jesus.
But the fruit of the Spirit is love, joy, peace, patience, kindness, goodness, faithfulness, gentleness and self-control (Galatians 5:22–23).

GREAT IS THE LORD!

Great is the Lord and the presence of His Spirit so mighty:
>bringing fruit of love, joy, peace, patience, kindness, goodness, faithfulness, gentleness and self-control to each believer;
>bringing gifts in many forms, all distributed so that the church, the body of Christ, may be complete;
>bringing the grace of God into our lives each moment of the day!

And what does the Lord my God require of me to receive such bounty?
That I love Him:
>love Him with all my heart,
>love Him with all my soul,
>love Him with all my mind, and
>love Him with all my strength.

Oh, how great is the Lord!

>"In the last days," God says, "I will pour out my Spirit on all people" (Acts 2:17).

GOD'S POWER IN US

To know God's power, cry out for God's purity.

> Have mercy on me, O God, according to your unfailing love; according to your great compassion blot out my transgressions.
> Wash away all my iniquity and cleanse me from my sin (Psalm 51:1-2).

To know God's power, yearn for God's presence.

> How lovely is your dwelling place, O LORD Almighty! My soul yearns, even faints, for the courts of the LORD; my heart and my flesh cry out for the living God (Psalm 84:1-2).

To know God's power, live with the risen, glorified Christ.

> For to be sure, he was crucified in weakness, yet he lives by God's power. Likewise, we are weak in him, yet by God's power we will live with him to serve you (2 Corinthians 13:4).

WHAT JOY!

What joy to be in the presence of God;
    what joy to walk with Jesus;
    what joy to be filled with the Holy Spirit;
    what joy to know the three are One!

> "Jesus Christ has received from the Father the promised Holy Spirit and has poured out what you now see and hear" (Acts 2:33).

ONE TRUTH?

2 + 2 = 0	Atheists say, "There is no God."
2 + 2 = 1	Buddhists find truth within.
2 + 2 = 2	Hindus find truth in reincarnation.
2 + 2 = 3	Judaism waits for the Messiah.
2 + 2 = 4	Jesus said, "I am the way and the truth and the life. No one comes to the Father except through me" (John 14:6).
2 + 2 = 5	Mormons add the revelation of Joseph Smith to the Gospel of Jesus.
2 + 2 = 6	Muslims believe Mohammed and the Koran surpass Jesus and the Bible.
2 + 2 = everything	New Age believers say, "All is God."
2 + 2 = anything	Unity believers have many paths to God.

Can there be only one truth?

ENTERING IN!

Entering in:

> His Presence is one of complete purity, dazzling white, not one spot of impurity or sin;
>
> His Presence fills the throne room, fills the earth and sky, fills the heavens;
>
> His Presence embraces all that was, all that is, all that will be.

Only those who are cleansed by the blood of the Lamb, Jesus Christ, can enter into His Presence.

Praise the Lord!

> Jesus' clothes became dazzling white, whiter than anyone in the world could bleach them (Mark 9:3).

HIS WORD

Reading God's Word leads to praying to God.
Praying to God leads to resting in God.
Resting in God leads to knowing God's will.
Knowing God's will leads to knowing God's way.
Knowing God's way leads to knowing God's time.
Knowing God's time leads to fulfillment of God's will.
Fulfillment of God's will brings glory to God.

And it all starts with His Word.

Your word is a lamp to my feet and a light to my path
(Psalm 119:105).

YOUR WORD

Your Word, O God, is …
    perfect,
    trustworthy,
    right,
    radiant,
    pure,
    and firm.

Your Word, O God, …
    refreshes the soul;
    makes wise the simple;
    gives joy to the heart;
    gives light to the eyes;
    endures forever;
    is altogether righteous.

Your Word, O God, is …
    more precious than gold,
    and sweeter than honey.
    By it your servant is warned;
    in keeping it there is great
    reward.

Based on Psalm 19:7-11

WAITING & LISTENING

BE STILL

I sought to do God's will,

and God said, "Be still."

I tried to accomplish the plans I had laid out.

But God said, "Be still."

I sought all manner of ways and all types of advice to achieve my goals.

But God said, "Be still."

I pined over the glory of past accomplishments;

I paced the room like a caged animal;

I cried out to the Lord, "This cannot be your will!"

But the God said, "Be still."

> "Be still, and know that I am God; I will be exalted among the nations, I will be exalted in the earth" (Psalm 46:10).

CROSSING THE DESERT

O Lord, why are You so far off? I am like a wanderer in the desert knowing only a mirage of Your Spirit.

O Lord, come soon, so that I may reach the refreshing oasis of Your presence.

May I not be put to shame; may others not be able to say, "He searched in vain to follow the Lord."

> In this you greatly rejoice, though now for a little while you may have had to suffer grief in all kinds of trials. These have come so that your faith—of greater worth than gold, which perishes even though refined by fire—may be proved genuine (1 Peter 1:6-7).

MY COMPLAINT TO GOD

I wait for You Lord,
    maybe not patiently,
    maybe not lovingly,
    but I wait.

I call on Your Name,
    but it seems as if You do not answer my calls,
    do not respond to my letters,
    do not give me an appointment.

I pray to You in despair,
    confess my sins as I know them,
    in private to You and to others who believe,
    and yet You remain silent.

Am I to say, "God is not there!"?
    am I to say, "I can wait no longer."?
    No, I know You are there, Lord,
    and I know that You care,
    also I know that Your will will be done.

I will wait Lord, but remember Your servant for I am in anguish.

> "If you have raced with men on foot and they have worn you out, how can you compete with horses? If you stumble in safe country, how will you manage in the thickets?" declares the LORD (Jeremiah 12:5).

LISTEN TO THE LORD

If the Lord whispers, "Stop."—STOP!
    If the Lord whispers, "Wait."—WAIT!
        If the Lord whispers, "Go."—GO!
Listen to the whisper of the Lord.

> "How faint the whisper we hear of him!"
> (Job 26:14).

WAIT FOR THE LORD

Wait for the Lord!
> Wait with quietness and patience.

Wait for the Lord!
> Wait with joy and anticipation.

Wait for the Lord!
> Wait, listening for the softest whisper of His Spirit.

Wait for the Lord!
> Wait!

> Wait for the LORD; be strong and take heart and wait for the LORD (Psalm 27:14).

YOUR VOICE

I delight, O Lord, in your voice!
You speak to us through the scriptures from Genesis to Malachi, from Matthew to Revelation, that we may know You more, that we may love You more.

> Your word is a lamp to my feet and a light for my path (Psalm 119:105).

I delight, O Lord, in your voice!
You speak to us through Your Spirit, made possible by Jesus dying for our sins, that we may know You more, that we may love You more.

> "Whoever believes in me, as the Scripture has said, streams of living water will flow from within him" (John 7:38).

I delight, O Lord, in your voice!
You speak to us through Your creation: the heavens, even the highest heavens, and the earth with all its beauty, that we may know You more, that we may love You more.

> "Holy, holy, holy is the LORD Almighty; the whole earth is full of his glory" (Isaiah 6:3).

I delight, O Lord, in your voice!
You speak to us in answer to our prayers, that we may know You more, that we may love You more.

> This is the confidence we have in approaching God: that if we ask anything according to his will, he hears us (1 John 5:14).

I delight, O Lord, in your voice!
You speak to us through Your faithful servants, both those with us and the legacies of those with You, that

we may know You more, that we may love You more.

> It was he who gave some to be apostles, some to be prophets, some to be evangelists, and some to be pastors and teachers (Ephesians 4:11).

I delight, O Lord, in your voice!
You speak to us through fellowship with other believers in many diverse and surprising ways, that we may know You more, that we may love You more.

> And let us consider how we may spur one another on toward love and good deeds (Hebrews 10:24).

I delight, O Lord, in your voice!
You speak to us through the details of life and the wonderful "coincidences" that can only come from You, that we may know You more, that we may love You more.

> And God is able to make all grace abound to you, so that in all things at all times, having all that you need, you will abound in every good work (2 Corinthians 9:8).

I delight, O Lord, in your voice!
You speak to us through the events of each day: the joys, the sorrows, the victories, the defeats, that we may know You more, that we may love You more.

> And we know that in all things God works for the good of those who love him, who have been called according to his purpose (Romans 8:28).

I delight, O Lord, in your voice!
You speak to us, at times, through visions and dreams to fulfill Your purposes, and that we may know You more, that we may love You more.

> "I will pour out my Spirit on all people. Your young men will see visions, your old men will dream dreams" (Acts 2:17).

I delight, O Lord, in your voice!

Yes, even to hear You speak.

> "Speak, LORD, for your servant is listening"
> (1 Samuel 3:9).

MY WILL – HIS WILL

The will to trust.

> The will to obey.
>
>> The will to draw near.
>>
>>> The will to surrender all.
>
> The will to simply follow.
>
> The will to do His will.

Choose for yourselves this day: your will or His will. But as for me and my household we will serve the Lord.

>> Based on Joshua 24:15.

WALKING WITH JESUS

THE FIRST EASTER

It was a morning like many others.
   The dawn air was clear and cool.
   A light dew was on the grass.
   A peaceful quiet filled a world not yet fully awake.
   Birds sang in early morning chorus.
   Lambs bleated in the distance.
   Rabbits hopped to find their early morning food.

It was a morning like no other.
   A group of women went to the tomb to anoint His body.
   The stone at the entrance to the tomb had been rolled away.
   The tomb was empty.
   An angel appeared to them and said, "He is not here. He has risen!"
   Jesus Christ had risen!
   Satan had been defeated.

The world would never be the same.

   Based on Matthew 28:1-7 and Luke 24:1-8.

ABIDE IN HIM

Oh how difficult it is to abide in the Lord: difficult in times of great activity and difficult in times of low activity, difficult in times of forward progress and difficult in times of frustration, difficult in times of being honored and difficult in times of being criticized.

> To abide in Him is to recognize the deceit in our hearts.
> To abide in Him is to allow the Spirit of Christ to flow into our hearts.
> To abide in Him is to work diligently and responsibly for the Lord.
> To abide in Him is to wait quietly on the Lord.
> To abide in Him is to know that the pathway He blocks no one can clear.
> To abide in Him is to know that the doors He opens no one can shut.
> To abide in Him is to suffer through many trials and hardships.
> To abide in Him is to know that the Lord will not let us be tempted beyond what we can endure.

Then we find that His yoke is easy and His burden is light as all things do work together for those who love God. Amen.

> "Abide in Me, and I in you. As the branch cannot
> bear fruit of itself, unless it abides in the vine,
> neither can you, unless you abide in Me"
> (John 15:4 NKJV).

HIS PEACE

Know His peace,
    know His pace,
        by His Spirit,
            by His grace.

"Peace I leave with you; my peace I give you"
(John 14:27).

OUR CHOOSING

As we abide in Jesus we know His presence.
As we abide in Jesus we know His peace.
As we abide in Jesus we know His power.

> As we forsake Jesus we lose His presence.
> As we forsake Jesus we lose His peace.
> As we forsake Jesus we lose His power.

Oh, the joy of abiding!—Oh, the pain of forsaking!—each of our choosing.

> Today, dear Jesus, I choose to abide in You.

I have set before you life and death, blessings and curses. Now choose life (Deuteronomy 30:19).

LEAD ME ON

Lead me on, Lord Jesus, lead me on!

> Make my feet like the feet of a deer, to enable me to go on the heights. Broaden the path beneath me so that my ankles do not turn.

Lead me on, Lord Jesus, lead me on!

> Renew my strength so that I can soar on wings like an eagle, so that I can run and not grow weary, walk and not be faint.

Lead me on, Lord Jesus, lead me on!

> Help me strain toward what is ahead; to press on toward the goal to win the prize for which You have called me heavenward.

Lead me on, Lord Jesus, lead me on!

Based on Psalms 18:33 and 36, Isaiah 40:31,
and Philippians 3:13-14.

JESUS IS MY FRIEND

Jesus is my Friend.
>He wants me to be His friend:
>to walk with Him as His friend,
>to talk with Him as His friend,
>to trust Him as His friend,
>to love Him as His friend.

Jesus is my Friend.
>I am Jesus' friend.

And the scripture was fulfilled that says, "Abraham believed God, and it was credited to him as righteousness," and he was called God's friend (James 2:23).

FOLLOW ME

At times life can seem like walking through a minefield and the only way to safety is to follow closely in Jesus' steps. Jesus has to speak sternly to us at these times because He knows danger is lurking if we should turn aside.

> "O Lord, I am overcome. The pressures of the world overwhelm me like a tsunami crashing on the shore."

> "My child, I know the situation you are in, but you must remember: if anyone would come after Me, he must deny himself and take up his cross and follow Me. For whoever wants to save his life will lose it, but whoever loses his life for Me will find it."

> "O Lord, I am fearful. My mind is unable to find a path through the difficulties. Each direction seems to hold more dangers."

> "My child, you do not need to know the path because I know the path. You must follow closely to Me, however, because the man who loves his life will lose it, while the man who hates his life in this world will keep it for eternal life. Whoever serves Me must follow Me; and where I am, My servant also will be. My Father will honor the one who serves Me."

> "O Lord, I am terrified. Sleep escapes me. I toss and turn on a bed of apprehension."

> "My child, I know your weaknesses and your fears,

but you must hold fast to My teaching. My sheep listen to My voice; I know them, and they follow Me. I give them eternal life, and they shall never perish; no one can snatch them out of My hand. My Father, who has given them to Me, is greater than all; no one can snatch them out of My Father's hand. I and the Father are one."

Praise Him, the Good Shepherd, who leads us to safety, forgives our doubts and fears, and fills us with His abiding peace.

Based on Matthew 16:24-25, John 10:27-30 and John 12:25-26.

COME UP HIGHER

"**My** child, come up higher!"

"Come up higher in faith:
be filled to the measure of all the fullness of God, and
be strong in the Lord and in his mighty power.

"Come up higher in love:
live a life of love, just as Christ loved us, and
speak the truth in love.

"Come up higher in service:
live a life worthy of the calling you have received, and
serve wholeheartedly, as if you were serving the Lord.

"Come up higher in worship:
sing and make music in your heart to the Lord, and
give thanks to God the Father for everything.

"My child, come up higher!"

Based on Ephesians 3:19, 4:1, 4:15, 5:2, 5:19, 5:20,
6:7, 6:10.

YOU ARE TOO WONDERFUL

O Lord, You are too wonderful to me.

When I follow Your way,
> You are the light in my eyes,
> You are the glow on my face;
> You give me peace,
> You give me joy,
> You give me love;
> my spirit tastes the joy of being in Your eternal presence in heaven.

When I divert from Your way,
> my eyes go dim,
> my face no longer glows;
> my peace turns to distress,
> my joy turns to misery,
> my love grows cold;
> my spirit tastes the anguish of being eternally separated from You in hell.

O Lord, my heart's desire is to do Your will,
> to be the person You created me to be,
> to fulfill Your purpose for my life, and
> to live in the house of the Lord forever.

O Lord, You are too wonderful to me.

Praise be to the LORD, for He showed his wonderful love to me (Psalm 31:21).

JESUS A to Z

I pray that you, being rooted and established in love, may have power, together with all the Lord's holy people, to grasp how wide and long and high and deep is the love of Christ (Ephesians 3:17-18).

> Jesus is my Anchor.
>
> We have this hope of Jesus as an anchor for the soul, firm and secure. It enters the inner sanctuary behind the curtain (Hebrews 6:19).

Jesus is my Bread of Life.

Jesus said, "I am the bread of life (John 6:48).

> Jesus is my Confidence.
>
> Such confidence as this is ours through Christ before God (2 Corinthians 3:4).

Jesus is my Delight.

That is why, for Christ's sake, I delight in weaknesses, in insults, in hardships, in persecutions, in difficulties. For when I am weak, then I am strong (2 Corinthians 12:10).

> Jesus is my Encourager.
>
> May our Lord Jesus Christ himself encourage your hearts and strengthen you in every good deed and word (2 Thessalonians 2:16-17).

Jesus is my Fire.

Jesus will baptize you with the Holy Spirit and with fire (Matthew 3:11).

> Jesus is my Glory.
>
> Now if we are God's children we share in Christ's sufferings in order that we may also

share in his glory (Romans 8:17).

Jesus is my Hope.

God has chosen to make known the glorious riches of this mystery, which is Christ in you, the hope of glory (Colossians 1:27).

Jesus is my Intercessor.

Christ Jesus is at the right hand of God and is also interceding for us (Romans 8:34).

Jesus is my Joy.

You love Jesus; and even though you do not see him now, you believe in him and are filled with an inexpressible and glorious joy (1 Peter 1:8).

Jesus is my King.

Jesus Christ is Lord of lords and King of kings— and with him will be his called, chosen and faithful followers (Revelation 17:14).

Jesus is my Lord.

What is more, I consider everything a loss compared to the surpassing greatness of knowing Christ Jesus my Lord (Philippians 3:8).

Jesus is my Majesty.

We told you about the power and coming of our Lord Jesus Christ... we were eyewitnesses of his majesty (2 Peter 1:16).

Jesus is my good News.

Jesus said to them, "Go into all the world and preach the good news to all creation" (Mark 16:15).

Jesus is my One and Only.

We have seen his glory, the glory of Jesus the One and Only, who came from the Father, full of grace and truth (John 1:14).

Jesus is my Peace.

Let the peace of Christ rule in your hearts, since as members of one body you were called to peace (Colossians 3:15).

> Jesus is the Quality of my work.
>
> The fire of Jesus Christ will test the quality of each man's work (1 Corinthians 3:13).

Jesus is my Redeemer.

Our great God and Savior, Jesus Christ, who gave himself for us to redeem us (Titus 2:13-14).

> Jesus is my Savior.
>
> Grow in the grace and knowledge of our Lord and Savior Jesus Christ (2 Peter 3:18).

Jesus is my Truth.

I speak the truth in Christ (Romans 9:1).

> Jesus is my Universe.
>
> Jesus Christ ascended higher than all the heavens, in order to fill the whole universe (Ephesians 4:10).

Jesus is my Vision.

Paul said, "I was not disobedient to the vision [of Christ] from heaven" (Acts 26:19).

> Jesus is my Way.
>
> Jesus answered, "I am the way and the truth and the life" (John 14:6).

Jesus is my eXample.

Follow my example, as I follow the example of Christ (1 Corinthians 11:1).

> Jesus is my Yoke.
>
> Jesus said, "Take my yoke upon you and learn from me, for I am gentle and humble in heart, and you will find rest for your souls" (Matthew 11:29).

Jesus is my Zeal.

Never be lacking in zeal, but keep your spiritual fervor, serving the Lord Jesus (Romans 12:11).

> Jesus is my All.
>
> He is the Alpha and the Omega, the First and the Last, the Beginning and the End (Revelation 22:13).

Amen

TODAY'S REMINDERS

Today's Reminders:

- √ God is for me—know that He is Lord—glorify Him not myself.
- √ God is with me—walk minute by minute with Jesus—go His way not my way.
- √ God is in me—remain in the Spirit—exhibit the fruit of the Spirit not the fruit of my sinful nature.

But encourage one another daily, as long as it is called "Today," so that none of you may be hardened by sin's deceitfulness (Hebrews 3:13).

THAT I MAY LOVE YOU MORE

Dear Lord Jesus,
>   Show me who I am,
>   that I may know You more,
>   that I may love You more.
>
>> Take away my sins,
>> that I may know You more,
>> that I may love You more.
>
>>> Tear away my sins,
>>> that I may know You more,
>>> that I may love You more.
>
>> Leave only Your Spirit,
>> that I may know You more,
>> that I may love You more.
>
>> That I may know You more,
>> that I may love You more.

Amen.

>   If we claim to be without sin, we deceive ourselves
>   and the truth is not in us (1 John 1:8).

OUR SIN & REBELLION

CLEANSE ME

Dear Lord Jesus cleanse me of my sins:
of doing what I should not do,
of saying what I should not say.

> Dear Lord Jesus cleanse me of my sins:
> of not doing what I should do,
> of not saying what I should say.

>> Dear Lord Jesus purify me, sanctify me,
>> cleanse me of my sins.

Search me, O God, and know my heart; test me and
know my anxious thoughts. See if there is any
offensive way in me, and lead me in the way
everlasting (Psalm 139:23–24).

HE IS FAITHFUL

You tested me, O Lord, and my faith failed.
    I slid into the mire of my bad decisions.
    I saw no way out:
    to go forward was to increase my despair,
    to return seemed impossible.

I cried out to You, O Lord, and You heard my cry.
    You reached down and grasped my hand into Yours.
    You lifted me out of the mire of my sinfulness.
    You washed off all the dirt that clung to me.
    You set me back on the rock of Your salvation.

You are so good to me, O Lord.
    You are faithful even when I am unfaithful.
    You are God Almighty.
    I praise Your holy name.

> If the LORD delights in a man's way, he makes his steps firm; though he stumbles, he will not fall, for the LORD upholds him with his hand (Psalm 37:23-24).

OUR SIN & REBELLION

TURNING ASIDE

How I disappointed You so badly turning aside at the very end.
How I hardened my heart against You denying You as my friend.
How the pleasure of going my own way became so fleeting in the following days.
How the loss of Your precious presence left a void in many ways.
How I sought to find You again: my heart full of remorse and fears.
How I felt You were gone forever: my purpose, my hopes all left in tears.
How my thoughts descended downward, making each moment struggle and strife.
How the darkness coiled about me, until to die was better than life.
How You stayed my foolish action, bringing others to my aid.
How the voices of these people turned the tide as they prayed and prayed.
How You slowly revealed my sinfulness—wrong thinking that led to that day.
How You gave me understanding—all You asked was that I had followed Your way.
How You showed the depth of Your love, desiring to lead me on paths anew.
How You showed my need to love You, surrendering all and all to You.

The LORD is close to the brokenhearted and saves
those who are crushed in spirit (Psalm 34:18).

YES LORD, I WILL FOLLOW YOU

FAITH & LOVE

NOT BECAUSE I AM ABLE

I will love the Lord my God with all my heart and with all my soul and with all my mind: not because I am able, but because Jesus will enable me.

I will love my neighbor as myself: not because I am able, but because Jesus will enable me.

> I have been crucified with Christ and I no longer live, but Christ lives in me (Galatians 2:20).

JESUS IS LORD

Love the Lord your God with all your heart and with all your soul and with all your mind.

Jesus is LORD!

Love your neighbor as yourself.
Matthew 22:37 and 39

A LIFE OF FAITH AND LOVE

A life of faith...
    comes from a day of faith,
    comes from an hour of faith,
    comes from a moment of faith.
    Teach me, O Lord, to live each moment in faith.

A life of love...
    comes from a day of love,
    comes from an hour of love,
    comes from a moment of love.
    Teach me, O Lord, to live each moment with love.

Teach me, O Lord, to live each moment in faith with love.

> The only thing that counts is faith expressing itself through love (Galatians 5:6).

LOVE IS...

Love is Jesus living in me.

Jesus is love and His love is alive in me if I truly love Him. Therefore if I say, "I love Jesus," yet I do not love others I deceive myself and the truth is not in me.

If I love little it is because I love Jesus little.
If I love much it is because I love Jesus much.

Love is Jesus living in me.

God is love. Whoever lives in love lives in God, and God in him (1 John 4:16).

THE WIND OF THE SPIRIT

The ship *My Lord God Almighty* is ready, but the anchor is still set and the sails are still furled—even though the fair wind of the Spirit is blowing—for I am still in the waters of struggling faith trying to get to the ship.

The ship *My Lord God Almighty* is ready, but the anchor is still set and the sails are still furled—even though the fair wind of the Spirit is blowing—for I am still in the waters of clinging faith holding onto the side of the ship.

The ship *My Lord God Almighty* is ready with the anchor raised and the sails unfurled, and the fair wind of the Spirit is blowing. Now resting faith has brought me into the ship ready to embark on the journey of life for His glory.

"You of little faith," he said, "why did you doubt?"
(Matthew 14:31).

Based on insight by Dwight L. Moody.

THE PURPOSE OF LIFE

The purpose of life:
to live each day,
where God has placed me,
for His glory.

Many are the plans of a man's heart, but it is the Lord's purpose that prevails (Proverbs 19:21).

YES LORD, I WILL FOLLOW YOU

REJOICE!

Rejoice! Jesus has risen allowing us to come freely into God's presence.

Rejoice! our prayers are heard because Jesus is interceding for us at the right hand of God.

Rejoice! Jesus has sent the Holy Spirit to guide us in all truth, and to guide us in our prayers.

> Christ Jesus, who died—more than that, who was raised to life—is at the right hand of God and is also interceding for us (Romans 8:34b).

THE BEAUTIFUL GIFT OF PRAYER

Thank you, Father, for the beautiful gift of prayer:

Thank You for prayer in solitude…
> "But when you pray, go into your room, close the door and pray to your Father, who is unseen. Then your Father, who sees what is done in secret, will reward you" (Matthew 6:6).

Thank You for prayer with other believers…
> They all joined together constantly in prayer, along with the women and Mary the mother of Jesus, and with his brothers (Acts 1:14).

Thank You for prayer in the details of life…
> Do not be anxious about anything, but in everything, by prayer and petition, with thanksgiving, present your requests to God (Philippians 4:6).

Thank You for prayer in the hard decisions of life…
> One of those days Jesus went out to a mountainside to pray, and spent the night praying to God. When morning came, he called his disciples to him and chose twelve of them, whom he also designated apostles (Luke 6:12-13).

Thank You for prayer at the start of the day…
> Very early in the morning, while it was still dark, Jesus got up, left the house and went off to a solitary place, where he prayed (Mark 1:35).

Thank You for prayer at the end of the day…
> After [Jesus] had dismissed them, he went up on a mountainside by himself to pray. When evening

came, he was there alone (Matthew 14:23).

Thank You for prayer with joy...
> I thank my God every time I remember you. In all my prayers for all of you, I always pray with joy because of your partnership in the gospel from the first day until now (Philippians 1:3-5).

Thank You for prayer with anguish...
> Going a little farther, [Jesus] fell to the ground and prayed that if possible the hour might pass from him. "Abba, Father," he said, "everything is possible for you. Take this cup from me. Yet not what I will, but what you will" (Mark 14:35-36).

Thank You for prayer with certainty...
> "Therefore I tell you, whatever you ask for in prayer, believe that you have received it, and it will be yours" (Mark 11:24).

Thank You for prayer with doubt...
> In the same way, the Spirit helps us in our weakness. We do not know what we ought to pray for, but the Spirit himself intercedes for us with groans that words cannot express (Romans 8:26).

Thank You for prayer by many...
> On him we have set our hope that he will continue to deliver us, as you help us by your prayers. Then many will give thanks on our behalf for the gracious favor granted us in answer to the prayers of many (2 Corinthians 1:10b-11).

Thank You for prayer by few...
> The prayer of a righteous man is powerful and effective (James 5:16).

Thank You for prayer with fellowship...
> They devoted themselves to the apostles' teaching and to the fellowship, to the breaking of bread and to prayer (Acts 2:42).

Thank You for prayer with fasting...

Paul and Barnabas appointed elders for them in each church and, with prayer and fasting, committed them to the Lord, in whom they had put their trust (Acts 14:23).

Thank You for prayer in all things...
Be joyful always; pray continually; give thanks in all circumstances, for this is God's will for you in Christ Jesus (1 Thessalonians 5:16-18).

Thank you, Father, for this beautiful gift of prayer.

MY PRAYER FOR YOU

> Our Father which art in heaven,

May you always look to God for guidance, strength and wisdom.

> Hallowed be thy name.

May you be in awe of God: in who He is, in all He has created, and in all He does.

> Thy kingdom come. Thy will be done on earth as it is in heaven.

May God's will for you in heaven become your life for Him on earth.

> Give us this day our daily bread.

May you trust boldly in God and His ample provisions.

> Forgive us our debts, as we forgive our debtors.

May you hold nothing against others and withhold nothing from God.

> Lead us not into temptation, but deliver us from evil.

As you face the struggles and temptations of life, may you always be victorious by seeking God's path to deliverance.

> For thine is the kingdom, and the power, and the glory, forever. Amen.

May you do all things to the glory of God. Amen.

Matthew 6:9-13 KJV

A PRAYER OF AFFLICTION

Abba, Father,
Oh that I learn to live within the limits of this affliction by heeding Your Spirit.
> Be joyful in hope, patient in affliction, faithful in prayer (Romans 12:12).

Oh that my days will not be cut short by failing to heed Your Spirit.
> "My spirit is broken, my days are cut short, the grave awaits me" (Job 17:1).

Oh that I bring glory to You by allowing Your grace to work through my weakness.
> But he said to me, "My grace is sufficient for you, for my power is made perfect in weakness" (2 Corinthians 12:9a).

Oh that I delight in my weakness as it is turned into strength by the working of Your divine power.
> That is why, for Christ's sake, I delight in weaknesses, in insults, in hardships, in persecutions, in difficulties. For when I am weak, then I am strong (2 Corinthians 12:10).

Amen.

PRAYER FOR THOSE SEEKING THE TRUTH

O Lord, these people are earnestly seeking the truth. Why should they go down to the pit?

> O Lord, many of Your children in Christ are not as earnest as these in seeking the truth.
> Why should they go down to the pit?
>
>> O Lord, have mercy on them.
>> Why should they go down to the pit?
>
> O Lord, may I live in Your light so that by Your light in me they may know the Truth.
> Why should they go down to the pit?

O Lord, hear my prayer.

> O LORD, you brought me up from the grave; you spared me from going down into the pit (Psalm 30:3).

MAY I THIS DAY...

May I this day not forget to pray for my family and those who are dear.

May I this day not forget to pray for my neighbors and those I meet along the way.

May I this day not forget to pray for my fellow workers: both the lost and the saved.

May I this day not forget to pray for the church, the pastors and my fellow believers.

May I this day not forget to pray for our country, our leaders and our government.

May I this day not forget to pray that I may walk humbly with my Lord and Savior, Jesus Christ.

May I this day not forget to pray.

> Then Jesus told his disciples a parable to show
> them that they should always pray and not give up
> (Luke 18:1).

WHY WE DO NOT HEAR FROM GOD

It may be that we do not hear from God because we do not want to.

> [The people] said to Moses, "Speak to us yourself and we will listen. But do not have God speak to us or we will die" (Exodus 20:19).

It may be that we do not hear from God because we do not take time to listen.

> The LORD was with Samuel as he grew up, and he let none of his words fall to the ground
> (1 Samuel 3:19).

It may be that we do not hear from God because of sin in our lives.

> If I had cherished sin in my heart the LORD would not have listened; but God has surely listened and heard my voice in prayer (Psalm 66:18-19).

It may be that we do not hear from God because we ask with wrong motives.

> When you ask, you do not receive, because you ask with wrong motives, that you may spend what you get on your pleasures (James 4:3).

It may be that we do not hear from God because we have other idols in our lives.

> Son of man, these men have set up idols in their hearts and put wicked stumbling blocks before

their faces. Should I let them inquire of me at all? (Ezekiel 14:3).

It may be that we do not hear from God because we hold something against another person.

> And when you stand praying, if you hold anything against anyone, forgive him, so that your Father in heaven may forgive you your sins (Mark 11:25).

It may be that we do not hear from God because something is wrong in our relationship with our spouse.

> Husbands, in the same way be considerate as you live with your wives, and treat them with respect as the weaker partner and as heirs with you of the gracious gift of life, so that nothing will hinder your prayers (1 Peter 3:7).

THE MANY PARTS OF PRAYER

What we usually think of as "prayer" is just one of the many parts of prayer.

Reading God's Word, the Bible, is part of prayer, as His Word draws us into His Presence.

Quietness is part of prayer, as we become still and know that He is God.

Speaking to God is part of prayer, as we lift our thoughts and voice to Him in adoration, confession, thanksgiving, and supplication.

Listening is part of prayer, as we anticipate His voice coming to us in one of many ways.

Preparing for the day's activities is part of prayer, as we invite God into the details of life.

Being receptive to the nudging of the Holy Spirit throughout the day is part of prayer, as He guides us through the maze of daily life.

Together these parts make praying continually a glorious reality in each believer's life.

> Be joyful always; pray continually... for this is God's will for you in Christ Jesus
> (1 Thessalonians 5:16-18).

IN SICKNESS & IN HEALTH

O that we would praise You and glorify Your name in sickness and in health.

> O that we would praise You in the joy of good health.
> O that we would praise You in the trials of sickness.
>
> O that we would praise You when healing comes through Your Spirit.
> O that we would praise You when healing comes through a physician.
>
> May Your name be glorified when sickness remains.
> May Your name be glorified when sickness leads to the final call home.
>
> May Your name be glorified through those who are cared for.
> May Your name be glorified through those who provide care.

O that we would praise You and glorify Your name in sickness and in health.
Amen.

> We pray this so that the name of our Lord Jesus
> may be glorified in you, and you in him, according
> to the grace of our God and the Lord Jesus Christ
> (2 Thessalonians 1:12).

YES LORD, I WILL FOLLOW YOU

OUR NATION

A PLEA FOR GOD'S MERCY

O Lord, I am a sinful man in a sinful nation.
> O Lord, many leaders of Your church have fallen into grievous sin;
> O Lord, many of the leaders of this nation too often act with evil intent.
> O Lord, how we have forgotten that it is You who has so richly blessed us.

O Lord, our only hope is in You; have mercy on us.

O Lord, may we not lose heart so that Your name can again be honored in this land.
> O Lord, may those who know You continually seek a closer walk with You.
> O Lord, raise up Spirit-filled men and women so that Your will can again flourish in this land.

O Lord, hear our cries!

> Blessed is the nation whose God is the LORD
> (Psalm 33:12).

O LORD, HEAL OUR LAND
Written during the Texas drought of 2011

Trees die, starved of moisture.
Fires rage through the dead and dying vegetation.

Similarly, hope dies among the people starved of Your Presence.
Fires of evil rage through the moral break down of our nation.

Even as the land cries out for refreshing rain from heaven, so we cry out for a refreshing of Your Holy Spirit from heaven.

We cry in shame of having denied Your living presence.
We cry for forgiveness of our sins of following the ways of the world.
We cry for a refreshing of Your Spirit to push back the evil and heal our nation.

O Lord, hear our prayers and heal our dry and thirsty land.
Amen.

> If my people, who are called by my name, will humble themselves and pray and seek my face and turn from their wicked ways, then will I hear from heaven and will forgive their sin and will heal their land (2 Chronicles 7:14).

CRY FOR OUR NATION

"**O Lord** Almighty God, You alone are God over all the kingdoms of the earth. You have made heaven and earth. Give ear, O Lord, and hear; open Your eyes, O Lord, and see; listen to the words Your enemies use to insult the living God.

"It is true, O Lord, that secular humanists, atheists, and others who do not honor Your Name have severely damaged the framework of our society. Even as termites destroy the frame of a house from within, so have they infiltrated the schools, the universities, the courts, the media and the government of our land intent on destroying our Christian heritage.

"Now, O Lord our God, deliver us from their hands, so that all kingdoms on earth may know that You alone, O Lord, are God.
Amen."

    Based on Hezekiah's Prayer in Isaiah 37:16-20.

MY WORKPLACE PRAYER

May I have faith to know You are always present to guide me in my work.

> May I have hope to know that my trust in You will not be disappointed.
>
>> May I have love towards all people I meet this day.
>
> May I remember that it is not for me to direct my own steps at work, but to follow Your way.

May I remember that it is not for me to seek power over others, but to serve others.

> May I remember that it is not for me to worry about tomorrow, but sufficient to do Your will this day.
>
>> May I know the peace and confidence that comes from following Your way at work.
>
> May I know the joy that springs from this peace as I see You move in the lives of those who love You.

May I know that all of this is possible as I pray and give praise in all things.

Amen.

Whatever you do, work at it with all your heart, as working for the Lord, not for men...
(Colossians 3:23).

THE BLESSINGS OF WORK

Think of work as a blessed task...
because through the trials of work we are drawn closer to God.

> Think of work as a vibrant opportunity...
> because by our attitude to work we can spread the fragrance of the knowledge of Jesus to those who are lost.

Think of work as having eternal significance...
because we can shine like stars in the universe at work as we hold out the word of life to those who need Jesus.

Based on 1 Peter 1:6 & 7, 2 Corinthians 2:14 and Philippians 2:15.

ALIVE WITH CHRIST AT WORK

If Jesus Christ is not alive in me at work today my faith is in vain.

Jesus is Lord of all my work today.
    I will praise Him today!
    I will trust Him today!
    I will rejoice today!

Jesus died for me so that I can live for Him at work today.

> We continually remember before our God and Father your work produced by faith, your labor prompted by love, and your endurance inspired by hope in our Lord Jesus Christ (1 Thessalonians 1:3).

THE JOY OF BUSINESS TRAVEL

Have joy when your flight gets cancelled.
Have joy when your bags get delayed.

Have joy when your hotel room is too noisy to sleep.
Have joy in situations that make you want to weep.

Have joy when your internet connection fails.
Have joy when your major client bails.

Have joy because God knows all these things.
Have joy because He will lift you on His wings.

"You yourselves have seen what I did and how I carried you on eagles' wings and brought you to myself" (Exodus 19:4).

I REJOICE

I rejoice in You, O Lord, my Comforter!
When I needed peace to wait through delays,
You gave me peace.

> I rejoice in You, O Lord, my Banner!
> When I needed strength to carry on,
> You gave me strength.

I rejoice in You, O Lord, my Righteousness!
When I needed humility to defer to another,
You gave me humility.

> I rejoice in You, O Lord, my Song!
> When I needed joy to encourage others,
> You gave me joy.

Acknowledge and take to heart this day that the
Lord is God in heaven above and on earth below.
There is no other (Deuteronomy 4:39).

HIS PRESENCE

Through the difficulties of travel across the time zones of the world: live in His all-embracing Presence.

> Through the stress of seemingly having more to do than time allows: live in His all-resolving Peace.
>
> Through the frustrations of being let down by work associates: live in His all-surrounding Protection.
>
> Through the physical demands beyond your capacity to fulfill: live in His all-sufficient Power.

Praise His Presence!
Praise His Peace!
Praise His Protection!
Praise His Power!

> "My Presence will go with you, and I will give you rest" (Exodus 33:14b).

YES LORD, I WILL FOLLOW YOU

THE LORD OF ALL CREATION

He led me to look to the heavens and His creation in the stars.

> He led me away from the city lights to see the awesomeness of the universe.
>
>> He timed this so that, as I watched, the stars faded and then disappeared with the approaching morning.
>
> He made me realize, even though the stars had gone from my view, they were just as surely there and shinning just as brightly.

He enlightened my heart to understand that it is so with His presence: in the time of morning devotions He seems so near, but then as the pressures of the day come upon us He seems to fade and disappear.

> Yet, He is there, just as surely and brightly as the stars are there, to guide us and guard us through the day.

For since the creation of the world God's invisible qualities—his eternal power and divine nature—have been clearly seen (Romans 1:20).

A REASON TO HOPE
Written at Hope, BC, Canada

The clouds were heavy on the mountain.
> I prayed to the Lord that He might lift them so I could see the awesomeness of His creation.
>> The Lord heard my prayers; the skies cleared and breathtaking vistas filled my view.

Again the clouds were heavy on the mountain.
> Again I prayed to the Lord that He might lift them so I could see the awesomeness of His creation.
>> The clouds remained, however.

I asked the Lord, "Lord, did You not hear my prayers?"
> He replied, "Yes, my child, I heard your prayers, but you must learn to see My presence in the dark days as well as in the bright shining days."

> "He causes his sun to rise on the evil and the good, and sends rain on the righteous and the unrighteous" (Matthew 5:45b).

THE BAY
Written at San Francisco, CA

Praise Him for the blue waters of the bay.
Praise Him for the grassy headlands.
Praise Him for the clearing fog.
Praise Him for the slumbering sea lions.
Praise Him for the diving birds.
Praise Him for all He has made.
Praise Him, praise Him, praise Him!

> Praise Him for the bridge that spans the entrance to the bay.
> Praise Him for the tower that opens panoramic views.
> Praise Him for the ships that ply the waters.
> Praise Him for the sailboats that catch the ocean breeze.
> Praise Him for the wharfs that bustle with people.
> Praise Him for making us in His image that we are able to create these things.
> Praise Him, praise Him, praise Him!

Praise Him for the ability to see all He has made and all we have added.
Praise Him for the ability to speak of His mighty wonders and how wonderfully He has made us.
Praise Him, praise Him, praise Him!

> Then God said, "Let us make man in our image..."
> (Genesis 1:26a).

THE MOUNTAIN LAKE
Written at Crater Lake, OR

The beautiful lake lifted high in the mountains reminds me of how Jesus was lifted high and exalted to bring the good news of salvation.

> The expanse of the deep indigo blue water of the lake reminds me of the expanse and the depth of Christ's love for all who believe.
>
> The vivid reflection in the still waters of the lake reminds me of how we are to reflect Jesus in our lives by the presence and power of the Holy Spirit.

The white snow touched with the crimson of the morning sunrise reminds me of how we, who are redeemed, are washed as white as snow by the blood of Jesus.

> That same day Jesus went out of the house and sat by the lake (Matthew 13:1).

THE BIRDS OF THE AIR
Written at Tewkesbury, Glos, England

The friendly robin, the lowly sparrow, the foraging pigeon, the brilliant gold finch, the busy blue tit, the shinning blackbird, the joyful thrush, the voracious starling, the distinctive magpie, the boastful crow, the heralding cuckoo...
>how they speak of Your love;
>how they speak of Your joy;
>how they speak of Your peace!

"Look at the birds of the air; they do not sow or reap or store away in barns, and yet your heavenly Father feeds them. Are you not much more valuable than they? Who of you by worrying can add a single hour to his life?" (Matthew 6:26).

COME AND SEE!
Written at the White Mountains, NH

"Come and see; come and see what My hands have made!

"See the bright red maple—the first to change its color!

See the varied colors of the sugar maple—green, yellow, orange and red!

See the northern red oak—its color changing to a warm dark brown!

See the aspen—still holding onto its summer green!

"See how the bright sun of the clear fall days shows the hillsides to be on fire with color!

See how the cool gray drizzle of the cloudy days brings a new richness to the colors!

"See, see what I have made that you may rejoice and be glad in My creation!"

> Let the fields be jubilant, and everything in them.
> Then all the forest will sing for joy; they will sing
> before the LORD (Psalm 96:12).

MAJESTY!
Written at Grand Teton and Yellowstone National Parks

Your majesty is on display:
> in the beams of evening sunlight piercing the clouds over the mountains;
> in a predawn opalescent blue to the sky that engulfs the mountains in a mysterious hue;
> in the fir trees once destroyed by fire now reborn to a fresh youthfulness;
> in the thermal geysers pouring forth—some predictably, others to a schedule known only to You;
> in the prismatic pools and springs displaying a palette of colors softly masked by rising steam.

Your majesty is on display:
> in a massive bull bison snorting and grunting orders to his herd;
> in a quiet heard of elk—the male standing proud with his grand crown;
> in a grizzly bear fearlessly walking alone, always watchful of his surroundings;
> in a reclusive female moose protecting her young as they feed in the swampy marshes;
> in the many small animals and a diverse array of birds—each with fine details made by Your hand.

Your majesty is on display:
> in knowing that all we have seen is just a small part of Your creation in this wonderful sanctuary.

> You are resplendent with light, more majestic than mountains rich with game (Psalm 76:4).

NOT BY CHANCE
Written at US Virgin Islands

Not by chance the pristine ocean water with shades of aqua, azure, turquoise, ultramarine and sapphire blues.

> Not by chance the varied sea birds: pelicans, gulls, terns, frigate birds, boobies and more.
>
>> Not by chance the curved bays with white sands, gentle waves, coconut palms and lush vegetation.
>
> Not by chance the blue sky dotted with fluffy white clouds and the occasional dark cloud to bring refreshing rain.

Not by chance such beauty; not by chance such variety.

> Only by You Lord, the Creator of beauty!
> Only by You Lord, the Creator of variety!

God saw all that he had made, and it was very good (Genesis 1:31).

FLOWERS OF THE FIELD
Written at Brenham, TX

Shout for joy! He is risen! The flowers of the field declare His praises!

The red phlox and the burgundy winecup declare Your victory over sin by the blood of the cross.
> The yellow daisies and the golden coreopsis declare the sunrise of the first Easter day.
> The pink primrose and the mauve foxglove declare the peace of the Holy Spirit You send to all who believe.

The blossoms of the bluebonnet and the bracts of the Indian paintbrush declare the great multitude worshiping You before the throne.

Shout for joy. He is risen! The flowers of the field declare His praises!

> The meadows are covered with flocks and the valleys are mantled with grain; they shout for joy and sing (Psalm 65:13).

TWO TRUTHS

The truth is revealed in God's Word, the Bible.
> All Scripture is God-breathed and is useful for teaching, rebuking, correcting and training in righteousness (2 Timothy 3:16).

The truth is revealed in God's creation.
> For his invisible attributes, namely, his eternal power and divine nature, have been clearly perceived, ever since the creation of the world, in the things that have been made. So they are without excuse (Romans 1:20).

Some say the truth revealed in God's Word surpasses the truth revealed in God's creation, and others say the truth revealed in God's creation surpasses the truth revealed in God's Word.

But there is one Truth that embraces the revelation of God's Word and the revelation of God's creation.
> In the beginning God created the heavens and the earth (Genesis 1:1).

Beyond this, we may not be able to fully reconcile the two parts of this Truth because God tells us:
> "For my thoughts are not your thoughts, neither are your ways my ways," declares the LORD.
> "As the heavens are higher than the earth, so are my ways higher than your ways and my thoughts than your thoughts" (Isaiah 55:8-9).

We can, however, boldly proclaim: "God is Truth in His Word and in His creation."

YES LORD, I WILL FOLLOW YOU

HIS VICTORY

HIS VICTORY

Jesus Christ our Savior reigns. His is the victory!
>His victory is when the nature of Jesus has uncontested ownership of our hearts.
>
>His victory is when we live to fulfill the purpose Jesus has placed in our hearts.
>
>His victory is when we follow the Way of Jesus rather than the way of the world.

Jesus Christ our Savior reigns. His is the victory!
>His victory is when we live daily in His presence with the fruit of the Spirit evident in our lives.
>
>His victory is when we live daily in His presence and His abundant grace in our lives.
>
>His victory is when we live daily in His presence with gifts of the Spirit bringing glory to God in our lives.

By this we witness of His love.
Amen.

>But thanks be to God! He gives us the victory through our Lord Jesus Christ (1 Corinthians 15:57).

THE LORD'S WARRIORS

Hallelujah, the Lord God Almighty reigns! His is the victory. We are His warriors.

In the clash of armies, the warrior must look to the Lord for guidance, for protection, for strength, for courage, for wisdom, for compassion, for rest, for healing, for recovery, for victory. So in our daily battles for the Lord, we must look to Him for these same things in our words and our deeds.

And as the battle rages, it is sometimes difficult to know if the Lord is there; sometimes it seems as if the forces that oppose us are too strong; sometimes it seems that those who are willing to fight for Him are too few; sometimes we wonder if it is worth going on.

But God is faithful. His victory is not by superior numbers. His protection is not by superior armor. His attack is not by superior weapons. The Lord's victory is His and His alone, made possible by His unfailing grace that can overcome all things.

> For the LORD your God is the one who goes with you to fight for you against your enemies to give you victory (Deuteronomy 20:4).

THE BATTLE

I desire to do Your will, my Lord, even with all my heart and all my soul and all my mind and all my strength—and yet I so often fail.

> Is it just my sinfulness, my Lord?
> or is it the sin of this world that also entices me from Your way?
> or, again, does the power of the evil one also seek to destroy my walk with You?

Often it seems that it is not just one of these evils, but all three battling against Your will for my life.

However...

With You, my Lord, there is victory over sin.

> He himself bore our sins in his body on the tree, so that we might die to sins and live for righteousness; by his wounds you have been healed (1 Peter 2:24).

With You, my Lord, there is victory over the world.

> In this world you will have trouble. But take heart! I have overcome the world (John 16:33).

With You, my Lord, there is victory over the evil one.

> Take up the shield of faith, with which you can extinguish the flaming arrows of the evil one (Ephesians 6:16).

With You, my Lord, victory is assured!

INCREASE MY FAITH

O Lord, increase my faith.
Fill the void in my armor lest I fall.

> Satan is pressing in at my point of weakness.
> The arrows of the evil one are aimed at the void.
>
>> I call upon you Lord and the victory You have assured.
>>
>>> O Lord, increase my faith.

Put on the full armor of God so that you can take
your stand against the devil's schemes
(Ephesians 6:11).

WHY SO FEARFUL?

Why so fearful, oh, my heart?
The Lord is my comfort and my confidence: the God of gods and Lord of lords!

> Why so fearful, oh, my soul?
> The Lord is my rock and my refuge: the great God, mighty and awesome!

>> Why so fearful, oh, my mind?
>> The Lord is my shield and my strength: the God of gods and Lord of lords, the great God, mighty and awesome!

> Yea, though I walk through the valley of the shadow of death, I will fear no evil: for thou art with me (Psalm 23:4 KJV).

THE GIFT OF TIME

Oh, the beautiful gift of time that God has given us, and that Satan, the prince of this world, so ferociously tries to snatch away:

>time to be with our Lord through His Word and prayer;
>
>time to live and work at His pace;
>
>time to see our Lord in the beauty of His creation;
>
>time to help those in need;
>
>time to serve our Lord as He stirs our hearts;
>
>time to be at peace with Him.

Yet our world and the prince of this world seek to rob us of this beautiful gift of time, urging us through our sinful natures to want ever more, ever more quickly, so that our hearts yearn for the things of this world rather than the living presence of our Lord.

The battle is real, the battle is daily, and we must engage the enemy with the full armor of God and the sword of the Spirit so that we can live victoriously with Him and not lose this beautiful gift of time.

>Teach us to number our days aright, that we may gain a heart of wisdom (Psalm 90:12).

GLOOM TO GLORY

"**My** child, why are you so disheartened and downtrodden? Do you not remember that your life is now hidden with Me in God? Do you not remember that you are a new creation in Me? Do you not remember you are alive with Me and you are co-heirs with Me?

"My child, take this into your heart and you will spread the aroma of My presence in your life; you will live as My ambassador; you will shine like a star in the universe as you hold out the word of life.

"My child, rejoice! You are more than a conqueror through Me. And rejoice again! You have victory through Me, your Lord and Savior Jesus Christ."

Based on: Romans 8:17 and 8:37, 1 Corinthians
15:57, 2 Corinthians 2:15, 5:17 and 5:20,
Ephesians 2:5, Philippians 2:15, Colossians 3:3.

PRAISE

LORD MOST HIGH

Praise You, praise You, praise You, Lord Most High!
   You turn my pride into humility.
   You turn my deceit into purity.

Praise You, praise You, praise You, Lord Most High!
   You turn my self-seeking into loving.
   You turn my self-keeping into giving.

Praise You, praise You, praise You, Lord Most High!
   You turn my worry into peace.
   You turn my woe into joy.

Praise You, praise You, praise You, Lord Most High!
   You turn my caution into action.
   You turn my weakness into boldness.

Praise You, praise You, praise You, Lord Most High!

> Look, the Lamb of God, who takes away the sin of the world! (John 1:29).

REJOICE, REJOICE, REJOICE!

Rejoice, rejoice, rejoice in Jesus our Savior.
Rejoice, rejoice, rejoice in Jesus our Lord.

> Though my heart faints within me,
> and Your way cannot be seen,
> I rejoice in Jesus my Savior,
> I rejoice in Jesus my Lord.

> It's not my strength that allows this,
> but His grace that is poured from above, so
> I rejoice in Jesus my Savior,
> I rejoice in Jesus my Lord.

Rejoice, rejoice, rejoice in Jesus our Savior.
Rejoice, rejoice, rejoice in Jesus our Lord.

*I will lead the blind by ways they have not known,
along unfamiliar paths I will guide them
(Isaiah 42:16).*

PRAISE HIM!

Praise Him, the One who anoints.
> You anoint my head with oil; my cup overflows
> (Psalm 23:5).

Praise Him, the One who blesses.
> The LORD blesses his people with peace
> (Psalm 29:11).

Praise Him, the One who crowns.
> He crowns you with love and compassion
> (Psalm 103:4).

Praise Him, the One who delivers.
> For he will deliver the needy who cry out
> (Psalm 72:12).

Praise Him, the One who enables.
> He enables me to stand on the heights
> (Psalm 18:33).

Praise Him, the One who fulfills.
> The LORD will fulfill his purpose for me
> (Psalm 138:8).

Praise Him, the One who gladdens.
> For you make me glad by your deeds, O LORD
> (Psalm 92:4).

Praise Him, the One who heals.
> O LORD, heal me, for my bones are in agony
> (Psalm 6:2).

Praise Him, the One who instructs.
> I will instruct you in the way you should go
> (Psalm 32:8).

Praise Him, the One who brings joy.

PRAISE

We are filled with joy
(Psalm 126:3).

Praise Him, the One who keeps.
The LORD will keep you from all harm
(Psalm 121:7).

Praise Him, the One who leads.
Lead me to the rock that is higher than I
(Psalm 61:2).

Praise Him, the One who has mercy.
He has heard my cry for mercy
(Psalm 28:6).

Praise Him, the One who meets our needs.
When I was in great need he saved me
(Psalm 116:6).

Praise Him, the One who ordains.
You have ordained praise
(Psalm 8:2).

Praise Him, the One who protects.
May your love and your truth always protect me
(Psalm 40:11).

Praise Him, the One who quiets.
He leads me besides quiet waters
(Psalm 23:2).

Praise Him, the One who gives rest.
My soul finds rest in God alone
(Psalm 62:1).

Praise Him, the One who strengthens.
The LORD is my strength and my shield
(Psalm 28:7).

Praise Him, the One who teaches.
Teach me to do your will, for you are my God
(Psalm 143:10).

Praise Him, the One who upholds.

> The LORD upholds the righteous
> (Psalm 37:17).

Praise Him, the One who brings victory.
> With God we will gain the victory
> (Psalm 60:12).

Praise Him, the One who washes.
> Wash me, and I will be whiter than snow
> (Psalm 51:7).

Praise Him, the One who exalts.
> He will exalt you to inherit the land
> (Psalm 37:34).

Praise Him, the One who renews youth.
> Your youth is renewed like the eagle's
> (Psalm 103:5).

Praise Him, the One who leads us to Zion.
> Sing praises to the LORD, enthroned in Zion
> (Psalm 9:11).

Praise Him from the beginning to the end.
He is the Alpha and the Omega.
Praise Him! Praise Him! Praise Him!

PRAISE

IN THIS I CAN REJOICE

In this I can rejoice!
I have hope in the Lord for today. He will guide me and guard me through the difficulties.

> In this I can rejoice!
> I have hope in the Lord for tomorrow. He will fulfill His purpose for me.
>
>> In this I can rejoice!
>> I have hope in the Lord for eternity. He will lead me home to the place He has prepared.
>>
>>> In this I can rejoice!

> Rejoice in the Lord always. I will say it again: Rejoice! (Philippians 4:4).

I SING TO YOU, LORD!

I sing to You, Lord. You give me:
love over indifference,
joy over misery,
peace over turmoil.

> I sing to You, Lord. You give me:
> patience over irritability,
> kindness over malice,
> goodness over immorality.
>
>> I sing to You, Lord. You give me:
>> faithfulness over fearfulness,
>> gentleness over harshness,
>> self-control over unrestraint.
>>
>>> I sing to You, Lord. You give me:
>>> the fruit of the Spirit over
>>> the fruit of my sinful nature.
>>>
>>> I sing to You, Lord!

Based on Galatians 5:22-23.

WHAT A PILGRIMAGE!

What a pilgrimage with Jesus by our side!

What a pilgrimage with the spirit of self replaced with the Spirit of God!

What a pilgrimage knowing the presence of the living God!

A pilgrimage that starts by being washed by the blood of the Lamb so that we can come openly before the throne of grace!

A pilgrimage that continues by being transformed by the renewing of our minds knowing the awesome presence of God the Father, God the Son and God the Holy Spirit!

A pilgrimage that forms a journey of life for His glory!

> Blessed are those whose strength is in you, who have set their hearts on pilgrimage (Psalm 84:5).

CONTACT THE AUTHOR

www.chrisjfenner.com
cjfenner@comcast.net
281-844-8366

OTHER BOOKS BY CHRIS J. FENNER

Following Jesus at Home at Work in all of Life

Following Jesus at Home at Work in all of Life is a twenty-six week study guide to draw you into an intimate relationship with our Lord and Savior Jesus Christ. This study will help you to: walk in the fullness of Christ (including the many hours spent at work); align your purpose with His purpose; make your life a continual witness to the lost and the saved; and experience that all things do work together for good.

Prayer Awakening: The Privilege & Power of Speaking With God

Chris Fenner's thoughtful book, *Prayer Awakening*, is practical and insightful. He helps the reader deal with real life struggles while offering useful reflections that will guide both the novice and experienced prayer warrior. If you desire to grow in the power of prayer and hearing God's voice you will enjoy this book.

The Day That God Cried

The heart of *The Day That God Cried* is the story of God's unfolding purpose for America since He created the world, and how He is grieving over our nation as we increasingly deny His living Presence in our culture and even in parts of His church.

Dire as our present circumstances may be, however, the Lord calls us to return to Him through a Spirit-led Awakening.

All the books are available at Amazon.com

YES LORD, I WILL FOLLOW YOU

www.ingramcontent.com/pod-product-compliance
Lightning Source LLC
Chambersburg PA
CBHW071518040426
42444CB00008B/1696